Friends of the Earth

Amy Rolf von den Baumen

"Soon it will be Earth Day," said Mr. Singh. "What do people do on Earth Day?"

"I know," said Jessie. "They do things to help the earth."

"That's right," said Mr. Singh. "There are many things people can do to help the earth. Do you want to do something to help?"

"Yes, we do!" said the class.

"Good," said Mr. Singh. "What can we do?"

"We could reuse and recycle things at school," said Kelly. "My mom says that too many people put bottles and cans and paper in the garbage."

"And they throw away things that could still be used," said Hui. "All that garbage takes up a lot of land!"

"We could clean up the creek," said Noor. "There's lots of garbage there."

"The garbage is bad for the fish," said Tom.

"It's bad for the animals who live near the creek, too," said Noor.

"I think we should plant a tree in the schoolyard," said Ann. "We need more trees."

"Trees do lots of things," said Trent. "They give us shade, and they're homes for animals and birds."

"We could watch our tree grow," said Ann.

"These are all good ideas," said Mr. Singh. "Which one should we do?"

"Recycle!" said Kelly and Hui.

"Clean the creek!" said Noor and Tom.

"Plant a tree!" said Ann and Trent.

"I know!" said Marco. "Let's do all three."

"We can get everyone in the school to help us," said Jill. "We can ask our families and neighbors to help, too."

"Good idea," said Mr. Singh. "We can do all three projects with help."

15

... APRIL 22

Friends of the Earth